Cover Picture: Gwennap Pit (17 miles from St Ives)
The pit was probably caused by mining subsidence in the mid-18th century. John Wesley preached to thousands at Gwennap Pit on eighteen separate occasions between 1762 and 1789.

In 1807 after his death the local people turned the pit into a regular circular shape with turf seats. In 2006, it became part of the Cornwall and West Devon Mining Landscape World Heritage Site. In 1744 John Wesley had described the pit as being, "a round green hollow, gently shelving down, about fifty feet deep; but I suppose it is two hundred across one way, and near three hundred the other."

Interesting fact: It takes two people 6 hours to cut the grass

Wesley's CORNWALL
A Pilgrim's Journal

Chris Huffadine

< Welcoming mosaic at the entrance to Gwennap Pit

Wesley's
CORNWALL
A Pilgrim's Journal

Wesley's
CORNWALL
A Pilgrim's Journal

Written with extracts from the
Wesley Journals and NIV Bible
by Chris Huffadine

The pilgrimages shown in the book are
available as a week-long series of walks and
visits from Christian Guild Holidays, based
out of Treloyhan Manor Hotel.

Quotations taken from John Wesley's Journals

Scripture quotations taken from the HOLY BIBLE, NEW
INTERNATIONAL VERSION, Copyright © 1973, 1978,
1984 by International Bible Society. Used by permission.

Ordnance Survey Licence: 100059447

< 21st Century
view of Warren,
St Ives

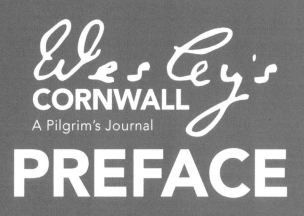

PREFACE

PREFACE

*Jesus said,
"I have come that they
may have life, and
have it to the full"*

John 10 :10

^ John Wesley
by John Faber
(1695-1756)
[Public domain],
via Wikimedia
Commons

Wesley's Cornwall is inspired by the Peak Pilgrimage (www.peakpilgrimage.org.uk) which leads the pilgrim through the Peak District from Ilam to the village of Eyam where the residents chose to give their lives to prevent the spread of the plague in 1665. We are indebted to Bob Jackson who devised the Peak Pilgrimage and who with a team of willing helpers published an excellent book to guide the pilgrims on their way. The Peak Pilgrimage is undertaken regularly from a Christian Guild Hotel, Willersley Castle. This booklet leads the pilgrim on a different journey through the life of John Wesley; a man who spent his life to save others from a worse death. John Wesley devoted his life to making known the saving power of Jesus.

This book has been put together to help the pilgrim understand more fully the 18th century environment, the life of John Wesley, his inspiration, and the roots of Methodism. It guides through parts of West Cornwall that were first visited by John Wesley between 1743 and 1789, a period of great change spanning nearly half a century. His ministry in Cornwall started with the angry mobs, and anxious clergy, who had their minds set on a ditty, first set in motion by the presence of John's brother Charles a few months before John's first visit:

"Charles Wesley is come to town,
To try if he can pull the churches down."

John Wesley's mind was, however, set on:
Do all the good you can,
By all the means you can,
In all the ways you can,
In all the places you can,
At all the times you can,
To all the people you can,
As long as ever you can.

Four years later he was able to say, "How strangely has one year changed the scene in Cornwall. This is now a peaceable, nay honourable station. They give us good words almost every place." This pilgrimage is not so much about the man as the message.

Jesus said, "I have come that they may have life, and have it to the full."
John 10:10

ICE CREAM AND
CHIP THIEVES
OPERATE IN THIS AREA
SHIELD YOUR FOOD

BEWARE THE GULLS

DON'T FEED THEM · DON'T TEACH THEM St.Ives

CORNWALL

A Pilgrim's Journal

INTRODUCTION

I lift up my eyes to the hills – where does my help come from? My help comes from the LORD the Maker of heaven and earth. He will not let your foot slip – he who watches over you will not slumber; indeed, he who watches over Israel will neither slumber nor sleep. The LORD watches over you – the LORD is your shade at your right hand; the sun will not harm you by day, nor the moon by night. The LORD will keep you from all harm – he will watch over your life; the LORD will watch over your coming and going both now and for evermore.

Psalm 121

INTRODUCTION

"I look upon the whole world as my parish; thus far I mean that in whatever part of it I am, I judge it meek right and my bounden duty to declare unto all who are willing to hear, the glad tidings of salvation"

^ Derelict mine on the 18 mile ancient trail between St Ives and St Just known as 'The Tinner's Way'

John Wesley first rode into Cornwall in 1743. Forty-six years later he preached his last Cornish sermon to thousands at Gwennap Pit, at the age of 86. His journal records, "My voice cannot now command the still increasing multitude. It was supposed they were now five and twenty thousand." His voice had held out for around 40,000 sermons! He visited Cornwall at least 32 times and visited many places more than once.

A snapshot of the many other parts of Great Britain where he had preached would reveal a very similar pattern. He visited Scotland 22 times. It is worth noting that Cornwall was only a part of what he called his "Parish". In all, it is reckoned, he travelled over 250,000 miles during his lifetime, either on horseback, in a carriage, or walking when it was all too much for the horse.

Our pilgrimage cannot hope to cover all the events and places affected by his ministry in Cornwall. It is therefore, focussed on some of his activities in and around St. Ives. There are some 326 miles of coast around Cornwall. Our pilgrimage takes us along a small part of the beautiful South West Coastal Path to just some of the most westerly places that John Wesley visited. After all, he spent most of his time in Cornwall in the west of the county, where mining was the boom industry.

John Wesley did not bring about the great awakening by himself. It had been a Bristol sea-captain, Charles Wesley and a couple of other lay preachers who had first ventured, from Wesley's society, into St Ives and the west of Cornwall earlier in 1743. It would be easy in our short time to be distracted from the geography of West Cornwall and also onto other preachers of influence; Charles Wesley, Billy Bray (who would walk along proclaiming "Glory" and "Hallelujah" every step that he took!) and lots of others. Many of them were unsung and have no books written about their endeavours. People like John Slocum who was a "poor baker's boy", dragged away to prison by his uncle for no good reason, but who later became an itinerant preacher in Cornwall. John Wesley said of him upon his death in 1777, "He was an old labourer, worn out in the service of his Master". We will not be distracted but keep our focus on John Wesley and West Cornwall.

To his mother, Susanna, John Wesley was known as Jacky. To the world today he is often simply referred to as Wesley. Many of the old records refer to him as "Mr Westley". Purists continue to pronounce his name Wehs-lee.

W	EH	S	-	L	EE
win	p**et**	**s**o		**l**et	s**ee**

He was often called many unrepeatable names by those who came to heckle and throw mud and stones. For the sake of clarity, we will call John Wesley, simply, John. This also saves the embarrassment of mispronouncing his surname, when reading aloud.

He is not to be confused with his brother Charles who accompanied him on his early visits to Cornwall, but then spent much of his life composing at least 6,000 hymns and poems from his home in Bristol. John wrote a mere 180 hymns!

To understand the lifestyle of those thronged around the various places outdoors where John preached will give the reader a fuller experience of 18th century Cornish congregations, the animosity, outrage and finally full acceptance of the preacher and his message.

Fishermen, smugglers, farmers, and a variety of other poor people will have been included amongst the hearers, but miners and their families formed the greater proportion. Cornwall was rich in mining resource such as copper, lead, arsenic, and tin. Tin Miners were known colloquially as Tinners and John has been called "Apostle to the Tinners". They usually had to travel several miles to their mine, descend through the mine for around an hour, do a very hard twelve hour's labour in the mine, and then surface and walk home. Many of the miners in this district will have walked

For the message of the cross is foolishness to those who are perishing, but to us who are being saved it is the power of God."

1 Corinthians 1:18

^ Abandoned
mine visible from
the South West
Coastal Path

The owre being with greate labor and charge gotten, requireth muche after-coste and trowble: firste it is broken with mightie hammers of iron; afterwards stamped to a lesser size with stamps headed with iron and raysed with a wheele which is driuen with the force of water. Then is it made farr smaller with a mill called a Crazing mill which grindeth it to a small powder; then it is washed with a mylde currant of water that falleth vpon greene turffes, carrying away the sande, and leauinge the mettall.

John Norden, 1584

along the Old St Ives Road between Morvah and Zennor. This road was known as Tinners Way. It is not surprising to discover that here, as elsewhere, John started preaching at 5 am. A time when miners and their families could stop and listen.

The breakneck work / life balance did not belong exclusively to the Tinners. Their wives and children would also work for the wealthy mine owners. Wives were called Bal Maidens (Bal is an ancient Cornish word for mining place) and were employed on the surface breaking apart the granite to extract the small quantities of precious metals. Boys over the age of eight also worked down the mine barrowing the extracted rocks along the 4 feet 6-inch-high passageways. The older miners would graduate to lifting the heavy ore to the surface by use of ladders. They would inevitably work from the bottom of the ladder, passing the ore up to men at a higher level. In other words they would get their foot on the first rung of the ladder. In time they would progress to working higher up the ladder. Their life expectancy in this extremely harsh environment was short, with few being fit to work beyond thirty or forty years of age. Disease was rife,

Tuberculosis, Bronchitis, and Rheumatism were common for those working in the dusty, barely breathable and extreme heat of the mines. Temperatures could reach as high as 60° Centigrade, and miners would sometimes work in the dark to save further pollution, from their bought candles.

John was a man who was gifted in communication. He could talk just as easily to masses of rough-tough miners, as to the gentry.

Again, I looked and saw all the oppression that was taking place under the sun: I saw the tears of the oppressed – and they have no comforter; power was on the side of their oppressors – and they have no comforter.

Ecclesiastes 4:1

^ James Pigot
and Co. Map of
Cornwall (1842)
[Public domain],
via Wikimedia
Commons

Some of the many places visited by John Wesley in Cornwall

Bodmin, Breage, Cambourne, Camelford, Carharrack, Carn Brea, Cubert, Falmouth, Goldsithney, Gulval (aka Trevarrack), Gwennap Pit, Gwithian, Hayle, Hellesveoar, Hilary Downs (aka Higher Downs), Holywell Bay, Illogan, Isles of Scilly, Kenneggy Downs, Kenwyn, Land's End, Laneast, Launceston, Lelant Downs, Liskeard, Luxulyan, Madron, Marazion, Mitchell, Morvah, Mullion, North Tamerton, Paul, Penponds, Penryn, Penzance, Perranwell, Polperro, Porkellis, Port Isaac, Poundstock, Redruth, Roche, Rosemergy, Saltash, Sithney, St Agnes, St Austell, St Buryan, St Endellion, St Ewe, St Gennys, St Ives, Stithians, St Just, St Michael's Mount, St Stephen's Coombe, Tredinney, Tresmeer, Trevean, Trewalder, Trewilhen Downs, Trewint, Trewoon, Truro, Wall, Warbstow Burrow, Week St Mary, Wendron, Zennor.

Coast Path

ZENNOR 3MILES

ST. IVES 3.5MILES

RIVER COVE
& FIELD PATH

< Waymarker on
the Coastal Path

Wesley's CORNWALL
A Pilgrim's Journal

JOHN WESLEY'S LIFE

JOHN WESLEY'S LIFE

"I learned more about Christianity from my mother than from all the theologians in England."

Train a child in the way he should go, and even when he is old he will not turn from it.

Proverbs 22:6

He was born John Benjamin Wesley on 17 June 1703 at Epworth Lincolnshire. He was the second son and fifteenth child of nineteen born to Reverend Samuel Wesley and Susanna ("Sukey") Wesley. Only ten of the children lived beyond infancy. Charles, his younger brother, and eighteenth child was born on 18 December 1707.

Susanna, who herself was one of twenty-five children, had a great influence on his upbringing. She schooled all the children six hours a day and had special time once a week for each of them. John's turn was on a Thursday. With so much going on around her in a busy rectory with lots of young children she would signal to them that she was not to be disturbed, during her times of prayer, by putting her apron over her head. The children were to be quiet during Family Worship, and along with many other rules for the household, they were taught to pray as soon as they could speak.

There are many women in history like Susanna who have had a significant input into the young lives of great people. Such was the maid Maria Milles a hundred years later who brought up the reformer Lord

Susanna's House Rules

1. No eating between meals

2. In bed by 8 p.m. (starting with the youngest)

3. Take medicine without complaining

4. Self-will to be subdued

5. To pray as soon as able to speak

6. Be still during Family Worship

7. Nothing cried for will be given

8. No punishment for faults confessed

9. Wilful disobedience or wrongdoing punished

10. Fear the rod

11. No punishment twice for a single offence

12. Comment and reward good behaviour

13. Attempts to please commended

14. Preserve property rights

15. Strictly observe all promises

16. No daughter to work before she can read well

Shaftesbury to, "Seek first the Kingdom of God".

Samuel and Susanna had a difficult relationship with spells apart. At least one of the absences was because Samuel was sent to Debtors' Prison.

Difficulties extended beyond the parent's turbulent relationship. One night in February 1709 when John was aged just five, the family home burned down. One of the upper rooms of the thatched rectory caught fire. The fire quickly spread, and John was trapped alone in his bedroom. He recorded later, "I saw streaks of fire, on the top of my room. I got up and ran to the door but could get no further; all the floor beyond it being ablaze. I then climbed up on a chest which stood near the window." The rest of the family escaped, but so severe was the fire that, after John's father had determined that rescue was impossible, he knelt and commended John's soul to God. Some neighbours saw that John had climbed up on to the chest by the window and they managed to grab him from the fire by standing on one another's shoulders. John later referred to his having been, "A brand plucked out of the burning", a reference to Zechariah 3:2. At the sight of his house in ashes, and all his worldly possessions up in smoke, Samuel cried out in joy and called his neighbours to give thanks to God, he said, "He has given me all eight children. Let the house go. I am rich enough." God had plans for John.

Home schooling stopped until the new rectory was built, during which time Susanna was upset about the way others influenced her children. At the age of ten John was sent to Charterhouse where he was taught Latin and Greek and attended chapel every day. John was bright enough to receive a grant at the age of seventeen to enter Christ Church Oxford.

John studied hard but also enjoyed swimming, boating, billiards, backgammon, tennis, and shooting. He had an interest in medicine as well as theology and the classics. This led him in later life to write a medical manual called, "Primitive Physic" which was so popular it was republished 23 times. Helpful advice such as using dried-powdered-toad to ease asthma, was one of the remedies! He also wrote about marriage, music, abolitionism and politics.

His self-evaluation in 1725 while at Oxford was:

- Too much addicting myself to light behaviour at all times;
- Listening too much to idle talk, and reading vain plays and books;
- Idleness;
- Want of due consideration in whose presence I am.

He determined to put things right, to the point that by the time of his ordination as a Priest in the Anglican Church in 1728, he was increasingly serious in his manner.

1725 had seen him ordained an Anglican Deacon, and as a Fellow of Lincoln College Oxford in 1726. Charles who had started at Oxford in March the same year, only began to take his studies and his faith more seriously after a year or two when he

^ The rescue of the young John Wesley from the burning parsonage by Samuel William Reynolds.

joined with a couple of friends. They met together every week to read together, take communion, and keep to rules devised by the group. They were very methodical.

During this time John had been helping his father back in Lincolnshire as a curate in Epworth and Wroot, but in 1729 he was invited back to teach Greek at the college. Soon after joining the group of friends, which was now disdainfully called the "Holy Club", he took charge and began to organise the small group of four. George Whitfield, who was to greatly influence John in later life, also joined the group. They began prison visitation, and in 1731 John began a small school for poor children. So began a systematic approach to social action that in later years would develop into the founding of hospitals, schools, and universities, helping all sectors of society and spanning all ages; most still going strong today such as the charities "Action for Children" and "Methodist Homes for the Aged".

John had believed that by his living a wholesome life, self-denial, determination, devotion to theology and preaching that

He gives strength to the weary and increases the power of the weak.

Isaiah 40:29 – 31

he would be saved. After all, he had been baptised, rose every morning at 4, studied the scriptures, was earnest in prayer and started preaching most days at 5 am. His religion had been so precious to him for most of life up until the age of thirty-five that he must have felt, as a priest, he was good enough to reach the heaven he so often preached and wrote about.

The younger George Whitfield, who was to become a life-long friend, believed the same; but as he began to understand more about the crucifixion, he discovered that it was by faith that he would be saved, not by works. His new-found faith will have added to any doubts that John already had about his own salvation.

John's father died in 1735. He had a hard life as a vicar in a small parish with family problems and parishioners who didn't always like him. As he was dying he said to his son Charles, "Be steady, the Christian faith will surely revive in this kingdom. You shall see it though I shall not."

In 1736 John sailed from Gravesend with his brother Charles for Georgia, a new British Colony named after George II, which had been formed just two years earlier. He returned two years and four months later after what seemed in many respects to have been a failure. During his time in Georgia he found that he was not accepted, and following some incidents, where he had strictly applied Anglican regulations, he found himself in an intolerable position with the judiciary, and decided to escape the unfair administration of the courts. He was deeply disappointed that he had not been able to minister to the people of the colony.

However, as he had sailed to Georgia he had been challenged by a Moravian Christian who confronted him with some challenging questions:

"Do you know yourself?"
"Have you the witness in yourself?"
"Does the Spirit of God bear witness with your spirit that you are a child of God?"
"Do you know Jesus Christ?"
"Do you know He has saved you?"

Although John knew all the right responses, he had doubts. He was only able to say, "I hope he has died to save me."

"For by grace are ye saved through faith; and that not of yourselves; it is the gift of God, not of works lest any man should boast."

Ephesians 2:8-9

In the same year as he returned to England, 1738, he met with a young Moravian, Peter Böhler, who spoke about faith in such a way that John, although he argued against his new-found friend, began to believe that he did not have true faith. Immediately it struck into his mind, "Leave off preaching. How can you preach to others, who have not faith yourself? I asked Böhler whether he thought I should leave it off or not. He answered, 'By no means.' I asked, 'But what can I preach?' He said, 'Preach faith till you have it; and then, because you have it, you will preach faith.'"

John wrestled with the 'works versus faith' dilemma that he found himself in. He eventually gave up fighting and cried out, "Lord, help Thou my unbelief."

WEDNESDAY 24 MAY 1738

Wednesday 24 May 1738 was to become the most important day in the whole of John's life, a red-letter day! By the end of the day he would be born again, not of flesh, but of the Spirit of God. He famously records in his journal for that day:

*"In the evening I went very unwillingly to a society in Aldersgate Street, where one was reading Luther's preface to the Epistle to the Romans. About a quarter before nine, while he was describing the change which God works in the heart through faith in Christ, **I felt my heart strangely warmed**. I felt I did trust in Christ, Christ alone for salvation; and an assurance was given to me that he had taken away my sins, even mine, and saved me from the law of sin and death."*

The next morning, he experienced a new joy and recorded, "The moment I awaked, 'Jesus, Master', was in my heart and in my mouth, and I found all my strength lay in keeping my eye fixed upon him."

If John had not come to true faith on that evening in the Moravian Chapel on Aldersgate Street in 1738, then the world would be so much the poorer, and many thousands who have been saved would have been lost. Methodists around the world acknowledge the significance of that special day by celebrating "Aldersgate Sunday" each year on the Sunday closest to 24 May.

In 1739 John, with close friend George Whitefield, began "Field Preaching". His inspiration came not only from Whitefield but from a sermon he preached the day before. John's topic had been "The Sermon on the Mount". He recognised that this was, "One pretty remarkable precedent of field preaching." His text for this, the first of many thousands of field sermons, was prophetic of the great things ahead: "The Spirit of the Lord is upon me, because he hath anointed me to preach the Gospel to the poor; he hath sent me to heal the broken-hearted; to preach deliverance to the captive, and recovery of sight to the blind; to set at liberty them that are bruised, to proclaim the acceptable year of the Lord." (Luke 4:18) Who could argue, looking back, that this is exactly what he had been called to do!

John devoted his life to preaching the good news to the poor. In 1742, having been banned from returning to his childhood church in Epworth, he stood on his father's tombstone and preached to thousands in the graveyard over seven consecutive days.

John did not carry on the ministry on his own, he developed a structure within which others would be appointed to preach, carry on the work and be accountable. Local "Societies" were formed, they too were accountable.

Jesus' sermon on the mount - "One pretty remarkable precedent of field preaching"

To keep everything working as it should he held annual conferences where decisions would be made about what was, and what was not, permissible. For example, minutes for Thursday 28 June 1744, from the first Methodist Conference, show that a decision was made about the best way of spreading the gospel. On the following day rules for Assistants were developed. The third rule for example, was, "Touch no woman; be as loving as you will, but hold your hand off 'em. Custom is nothing to us." Many topics came under consideration at the conferences, which continue to this day.

John's advice to the preachers was, "Let the preaching at five in the morning be constantly kept up, wherever you can have twenty hearers. This is the glory of the Methodists! Whenever this is dropped, they will dwindle away into nothing".

In 1751 at the age of 48 John hastily married Molly Vazeille. He had loved Sophia Hockey in Georgia twelve years before, and Grace Murray just a couple of years previously. Neither of these romances had ended with the marriage he had hoped for. Sadly his marriage to Molly was a disaster! They argued frequently and finally separated in 1771.

He felt so ill in 1753 with what had been diagnosed as "galloping consumption" (Tuberculosis) that, to save elaborate praise after he was deceased, he drafted an inscription for his gravestone, it read, "Here lieth the body of John Wesley, A brand plucked out of the burning, Who died of consumption in the fifty first year of his age, And leaving, after his debts are paid, ten pounds behind him: Praying, God be merciful to me, an unprofitable servant."

Such was his condition that his brother, Charles, and friend George Whitefield also believed he was going to die. They prayed, and with the care and nursing provided by Molly and the wife of a generous banker, who accommodated them during the illness, he recovered. He was soon back in the saddle, and as was his custom, he would read and maybe even write at the same time as riding.

Methodism grew at a phenomenal rate as John and his co-workers travelled far and wide. John himself records in his journals amazing opportunities in all the counties of Great Britain, but significantly mentions,

WESLEY'S CORNWALL
JOHN WESLEY'S LIFE

London, Bristol, Newcastle, Lincolnshire, Manchester, Oxford, Yorkshire, Winchester, Liverpool, Durham, Kent, Cambridge, Bath, Norwich, and Cornwall.

John's ministry was a blessed one, and a blessing to many thousands down through the ages. He had come to realise that he was God's workmanship, created in Christ Jesus to do good works, which God had prepared in advance for him to do (Ephesians 2:10). Just like Caleb, who said he was just as strong at eighty-five as he was at forty (Joshua 14:10 -11), he declared in his old age, "I am as strong at eighty-one as I was at twenty-one, but abundantly more healthy, being a stranger to the headache, toothache and other bodily disorders which attended me in my youth. We can only say, 'The Lord reigneth!' WHILE WE LIVE, LET US LIVE TO HIM!".

When asked, at the age of eighty-five, to what did he attribute his health and long life, he replied:

- The power of God fitting me for the work to which I am called;
- The prayers of his children;
- Constant exercise and change of air;
- Never having lost a night's sleep, sick or well, at land or sea, since born;
- Having slept at command;
- Rising at 4 and preaching at 5 am;
- To having so little pain, sorrow or anxious care.

This last point might sound strange. He had had near death experiences in fire, sea, and illness, been abused by mockers who threw missiles as he preached, lived through serious breaks in friendship with some of his closest friends, and his wife separated from him. He had rare moments of depression, yet, he now possessed the peace that he had first seen in the Moravians who had travelled through the storms with him to Georgia.

Less than three years later, the mortal life of the man who had fitted his feet with the readiness that comes from the gospel of peace lay in his death bed. Some of his last words were:

"I'll praise I'll praise…"
"The best of all, God is with us!"
"Farewell"

^ Wesley preaching outdoors

"I could scarce reconcile myself at first to this strange way of preaching in the fields, of which he (Whitefield) set me an example on Sunday; having been all my life - till very lately - so tenacious of every point relating to decency and order, that I should have thought the saving of souls almost a sin, if it had not been done in a church,"

< Part of the
varied terrain on
the South West
Coastal path
between Zennor
and St Ives

Wesley's
CORNWALL
A Pilgrim's Journal

YOUR
PILGRIMAGE

"It is good to renew ourselves, from time to time, by closely examining the state of our souls, as if we had never done it before; for nothing tends more to the full assurance of faith, than to keep ourselves by this means in humility, and the exercise of all good works."

John Wesley

A pilgrim is an individual who journeys to a sacred place for religious reasons. When Christians go on pilgrimage they travel somewhere that is special to their faith. It might be to places written about in the Bible, such as where Jesus and the early Christians lived. It may be a place where a miracle once happened, or a saint is buried. Often the journey itself matters as much as being at the special place, because it gives the 'pilgrim' – the person on the journey – time to pray and think. During this pilgrimage we cross over

THE CHRISTIAN.   63.

HYMN 63.   8. 8. 6s.   *J. C. W.*

The Spiritual Pilgrim.

HOW happy is the pilgrim's lot,
    How free from anxious care and
From worldly hope and fear ! [thought,
Confin'd to neither court nor cell,
His soul disdains on earth to dwell,
    He only sojourns here.

<< Path to the beach from Treloyhan Manor Hotel
< Hymn by John Wesley

another well-trod pilgrim's path. It runs 12 ½ miles from Lelant in the North through to Marazion and St Michael's Mount in the South. This was a route used by pilgrims in ancient times when they were heading for St James' Cathedral in Santiago de Compostela in northern Spain.

Our pilgrimage takes us to places which were very ordinary until Christians started taking the good news of Jesus to some of the remotest parts of the land. John and his fellow preachers made this, and many other parts of the world, special places of transformation.

John Bunyan's pilgrim was asked at one stage in his journey, by some 'Friends', "Ah, good Christian, where are you now?" Shortly afterwards he was asked by another 'Friend', "But why did you not look for the steps?" There are many physical steps on our pilgrimage and you would be well advised to, "Look for the steps". The physical environment, the rugged coastline and the difficult steps will both challenge

"Where am I now?"

"Why do I do what I do?"

and delight, but the bigger challenge is spiritual and is, "Where are you now?"

This is an opportunity to ponder and reflect on life with deep questions like, why was John inspired to do what he did? And, to consider not only where am I, but also, why do I do what I do?

Think about what John did and where he went. Then with you own personal ponderings you may begin to understand the beauty of the spiritual landscape.

Each day presents a fresh opportunity to visit some of the local places where John Wesley preached. Three of the pilgrimage walks take you along the beautiful South West Coastal Path, through the area referred to as the "Tin Coast", all the way from St Just in the West via Morvah, and Zennor, and on the third day's walk to St Ives.

Saturday 17 September 1743 John records, "I preached at St Just and at the Land's End, where, in the morning,

Sunday, the 18th, I largely declared (what many shall witness in due time). 'By grace are ye saved through faith.' (Ephesians 2:8). The congregation at St Just was greatly increased, while I proclaimed to every convicted sinner, 'Believe on the Lord Jesus Christ, and thou shalt be saved'. (Acts 16:31). About one I preached at Morvah, on Romans 8:15, to the largest congregation I had seen in Cornwall. The society afterwards met, consisting of above an hundred members. Which of these will endure to the end? At Zennor I preached on Isaiah 53, feeling no weariness at all; and concluded the day with our brethren at St Ives, rejoicing and praising God."

This was not an extraordinary excursion since the previous Sunday he had travelled a similar 21-mile route (Sennen – Land's End – St Just – Morvah – Zennor – St Ives) involving around seven hours of preaching, praise and prayer.

Rather than the one day this took John, you can take three separate days; no Land's End and no preaching. But, he did have a horse. You will be walking! But, be warned, if it has been raining, it can be muddy.

^ The walk can be muddy. Don't get caught in the 'Slough of Despond'

Whatever is true, whatever is noble, whatever is right, whatever is pure, whatever is lovely, whatever is admirable - if anything is excellent or praiseworthy – think about such things.

Philippians 4:8

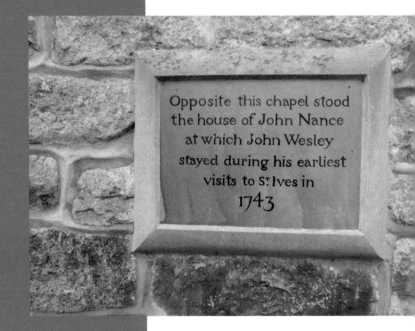

Opposite this chapel stood the house of John Nance at which John Wesley stayed during his earliest visits to St Ives in 1743

You may feel a little weariness, but spare a thought for John who would have been sleeping, till just four, at John Nance's house in the centre of St Ives with the threat of the rabble.

Indeed, Thursday 12 April 1744 John writes, "Between seven and eight the mob came and beset John Nance's house. John Nance and John Paynter went out, and stood before the door; though they were quickly covered with dirt. The cry was, 'Bring out the preacher! Pull down the house!' And they began to pull down the boards which were nailed against the windows. But the mayor, hearing it, came without delay, and read the proclamation against riots; upon which, after many oaths and imprecations, they thought proper to disperse."

NEW DAY PRAYER:

*"O LORD God Almighty,
Father of angels and men,
We praise and bless your
holy name for all your goodness
and loving kindness to humanity.*

*We bless you for our creation,
preservation, and for your
unceasing generosity to us
throughout our lives;*

*But above all, we bless you
for your great love in the redemption
of the world by our Lord Jesus Christ.*

We bless you for bringing us safe
to the beginning of a new day.
Grant that this day we fall into no sin,
Neither run into any kind of danger.

Keep us, we pray,
from all things hurtful to body or soul,
and grant us your pardon and peace,
so that, being cleansed from all our sins,
we might serve you
with quiet hearts and minds,
and continue in the same until our life's end,
through Jesus Christ, our Saviour and Redeemer.

Amen.

Based on the original by John Wesley

FIRST PILGRIMAGE
ST JUST TO MORVAH
5 MILES

St Just features often in John's journals. On Tuesday 25 June 1745 John wrote, *"We rode to St Just, I preached at seven. When the preaching was ended, the constable apprehended Edward Greenfield, (by a warrant from Dr Borlase,) a tinner in the forty-sixth year of his age, having a wife and seven children. Three years ago he was eminent for cursing, swearing, drunkenness, and all manner of wickedness; but those old things had been for some time".*

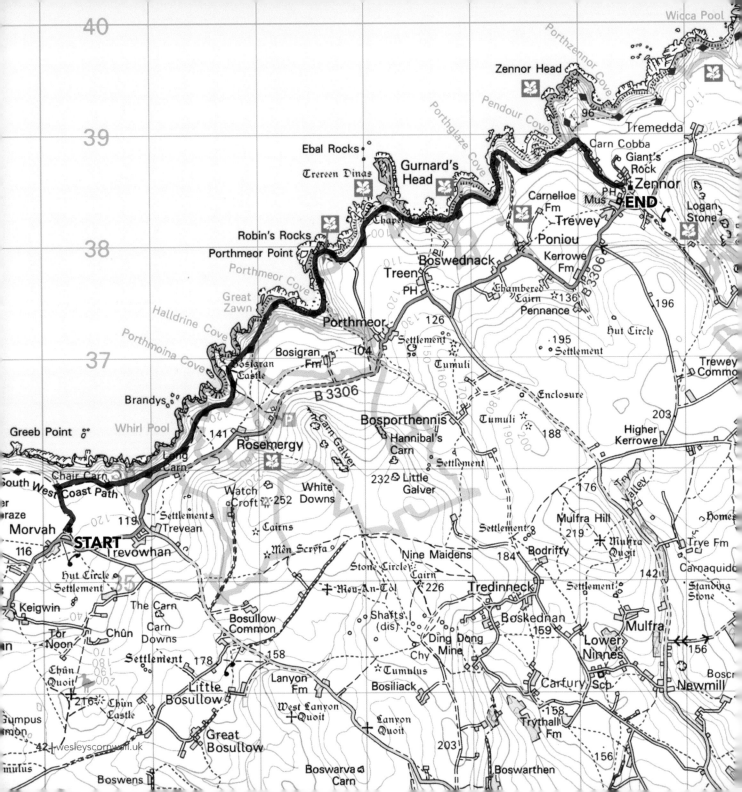

40

39

38

37

35

Wicca Pool

Porthzennor Cove

Zennor Head

96

Tremedda

130

Pendour Cove

Carn Cobba

Giant's Rock

120

Porthglaze Cove

Zennor

PH

Mus

END

Logan Stone

Carnelloe Fm

Trewey

Ebal Rocks

Gurnard's Head

Trereen Dinas

Poniou

Kerrowe Fm

B 3306

196

Chapel

Boswednack

Chambered Cairn

136

Robin's Rocks

Treen

Pennance

100

Porthmeor Point

PH

126

195

Hut Circle

110

Porthmeor Cove

120

Porthmeor

Settlement

Settlement

Great Zawn

104

150

Tumuli

170

Enclosure

203

Halldrine Cove

Bosigran Fm

160

Porthmoina Cove

Bosigran Castle

B 3306

Tumuli

188

Higher Kerrowe

Greeb Point

Brandys

Whirl Pool

120

141

Carn Galver

Bosporthennis

Hannibal's Carn

190

200

176

Try Valley

Long Carn

Rosemergy

Settlement

232 Little Galver

Chair Carn

P

Watch Croft 252

White Downs

Trye Fm

142

South West Coast Path

119

Settlements

Cairns

Mulfra Hill

219

Carnaquidden

Morvah

116

Trevean

Men Scryfa

Nine Maidens

184

Bodrifty

Settlement

Standing Stone

START

Trevowhan

Stone Circle

Cairn

Tredinneck

156

Hut Circle

Settlement

226

Men-An-Tol

Settlement

Keigwin

The Carn

Shafts (dis)

Boskednan

159

Lower Ninnes

Mulfra

Tor Noon

Chûn

Carn Downs

Ding Dong Mine

Carfury Sch

Newmill

Settlement 178

158

Chy

Chûn Quoit

200

Lanyon Fm

Bosiliack

Cumulus

Little Bosullow

Chûn Castle

216

Bosullow Common

West Lanyon Quoit

Lanyon Quoit

158

Trythall Fm

Boscr

Jumpus mon

Great Bosullow

Boswarva Carn

Boswarthen

203

156

42 | wesleyscornwall.uk

SECOND PILGRIMAGE
MORVAH TO ZENNOR
5 MILES

John preached many times at Morvah on the North side of the church. He wasn't allowed inside to preach. In 1743 alone he preached on the 2nd, 6th, and 11th September. On the 11th September he had a large congregation where, *"The spirit of the Great King was in the midst"*, and he was filled abundantly with *"Matter and words"*.

Today, the Schoolhouse Cafe, just over the road from the church is a great place for a cup of coffee where you can soak up a bit more of how he influenced schooling.

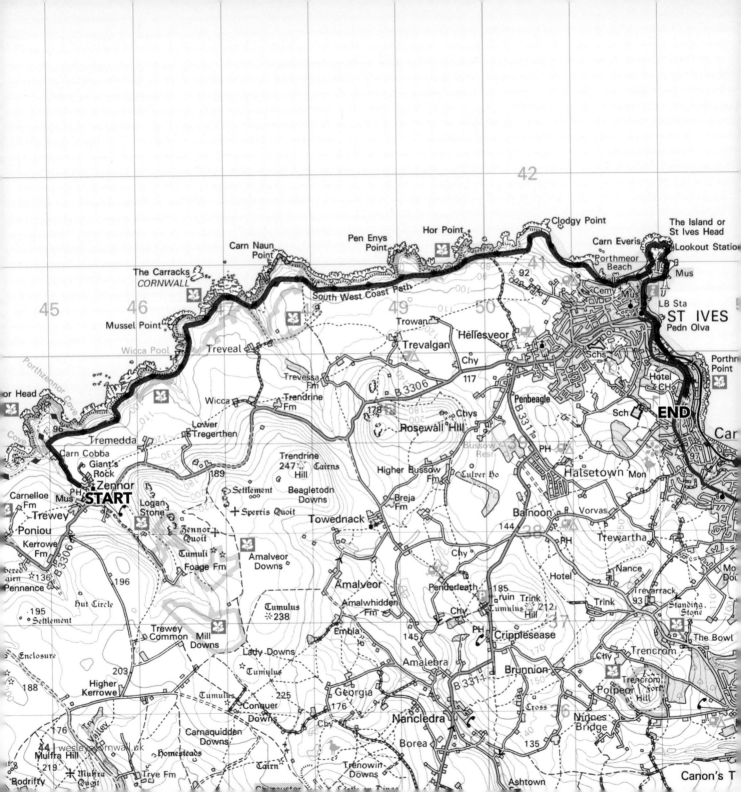

THIRD PILGRIMAGE
ZENNOR TO ST IVES
8 MILES

John preached by the church in Zennor and from on top of a rock at the top of the hill.

This walk takes a rocky route to St Ives. When arriving in St Ives stop to see the site of John Nance's house and the Market Place adjacent to the church where John met with so much opposition. There were many occasions where he met an angry mob in St Ives.

On Monday 18th July 1743 John records, "I went forth toward the market-house. When we came to the place of battle, the enemy was ready set in array against us. I began the hundredth Psalm, and they beating their drum, and shouting. I stood still and silent for some time, finding they would not receive my testimony: then offered to speak to some of the most violent; but they stopped their ears, and ran upon me, crying, I should not preach there, and catching at me to pull me down. They had no power to touch me. My soul was calm and fearless. I shook off the dust of my feet and walked leisurely through the thickest of them, who followed like ramping and roaring lions, but their mouth was shut. I met the Mayor, who saluted us, and threatened the rioters. I rejoiced at my lodgings in our Almighty Jesus." Later that day when he was preaching on blind Bartimaeus many of the opposers "trembled, and some wept". A week later the Mayor informed John and his colleagues that it was the Ministers who were the principal authors of all this evil, representing them as Popish emissaries, and urging the enraged multitude to take all manner of ways to stop them. The Minsters' preaching was erroneous and causing bitterness amongst the parishioners.

The day before John set out on his six day 300 mile journey back to London the drunken town clerk came with a drunken mob to John Nance's house, where John was lodging, intending to pull it down, but they were restrained by God, who at the same time caused John and the gathered society, by his power among them, to have hearts melted into contrite, joyful love.

Take a moment to stand where John stood in the Market place, and try to imagine the rioting.

If there is time then visit the museum near Smeaton's Pier to get a better understanding of Cornish life in the 18th Century.

< Waymarker on
the route from
Zennor to St Ives

> The mound
from which it is
believed John
preached

START

END

FOURTH PILGRIMAGE
ST HILARY TO MARAZION / ST MICHAEL'S MOUNT
3 MILES

On the 28 July 1743 John rode to St Hilary Downs and preached to Tinners, he wrote, "Here the careless hearers were kept away by the enemies threatenings; but near a thousand well-disposed tinners listened to the joyful tidings, 'Comfort ye, comfort ye my people,' &c. That the word of grace, 'Thine iniquity is pardoned,' quite melted them down into tears, on all sides". Again in 1744 he preached at St Hilary on Ephesians 5:14 "Awake thou that sleepest".

It was at St Hilary Downs where the popular, but false, legend that John lived on blackberries began. John Nelson, one of John's companions, wrote, "One day we had been at St

Hilary Downs, and Mr. Wesley had preached from Ezekiel's vision of dry bones (Ezekiel 37) and there was a shaking among the people as he preached. As we returned, Mr. Wesley stopped his horse to pick blackberries; saying, "'Brother Nelson we ought to be thankful that there are plenty of blackberries; for this is the best country I ever saw for getting a stomach, but the worst that I ever saw for getting food. Do the people think we can live by preaching?' I said, 'I know not what they may think; but one asked me to eat something as I came from St Just, when I ate heartily of barley-bread and honey.' He said, 'You are well off; I had thought of begging a crust of bread of the woman where I met the people of Morvah, but forgot it till I had got some distance from the house.'"

On the 9 September 1743 John returned to St Hilary Downs to find no congregation, but by the time he had put on his gown and cassock there were about a hundred gathered together to hear him preach on "repent and believe the gospel." He commented that, "If but one had heard, it was worth all the labour."

John's ministry was being carried out at a time of political unrest and uncertainty. People were being forced to serve in the army and navy, and around Cornwall many "able-bodied men without lawful calling or sufficient maintenance" were being pressed for fighting on the continent. John himself had been threatened in 1745 with a warrant to press him, "into the service of His Majesty".

In that same year he got news that Tom Maxfield had been seized while preaching. John rode with the rector of St Gennys to try and help, but before they got there Maxfield had been taken away to Marazion to appear before the magistrates. John waited there so that he could enter a plea for Maxfield. While he was waiting he climbed up St Michael's Mount and commented that,

^ The path near St Hilary Downs

"The house at the top is surprisingly large and pleasant, Sir John Aubyn had taken much pains, and been at considerable expense, in repairing and beautifying the apartments; and when the seat was finished the owner died!" John was not able to enter his plea because the magistrates heard the case without him being sent for. Maxfield was sentenced and after a short time in the dungeon at Penzance was sent as a soldier.

During John's last trip to Cornwall in 1789, at the age of eighty-six, he called in at Marazion, on his way to Penzance, where he had promised to preach once more. It was raining and, so he preached a short sermon in the new preaching-house which, "was considerably the largest, and, in many respects, far the best, in Cornwall." It was full within minutes.

"I build on Christ the rock of ages; on his sure mercies described in his word, and on his promises, all which I know are yea and amen."

John Wesley

< St Michael's Mount

FIFTH PILGRIMAGE
GWENNAP PIT & FALMOUTH

Gwennap Pit is probably the most famous place where John preached in Cornwall to thousands upon thousands of eager listeners. He liked to call this falling-in of an old mine working, "My amphitheatre". He preached there eighteen times between 1762 and 1789.

On 4 August 1744 he recorded, "I preached at Gwennap, where the awakening is general. Very many who have not courage to enter into the Society have yet broke off their sins by repentance, and are waiting for forgiveness. The whole county is sensible of the change; for last Assizes there was a jail delivery, not one felon to be found in their prisons, which has not been known before in the memory of man. At their last revel they had not men enough to make a wrestling-match, all the Gwennap men being struck off

< The small chapel at the entrance to Gwennap Pit

the devil's list, and found wrestling against him, not for him."

Stand on the edge of the pit and imagine the thousands whom John saw when he said in 1776, "I think this is the most magnificent spectacle which is to be seen on this side of heaven."

On 4 July 1745, soon after John rode into Falmouth, he went to see a "gentlewoman who had been indisposed". He wrote in his journal, "Almost as soon as I was set down, the house was beset on all sides by an innumerable multitude of people. A louder or more confused noise could hardly be at the taking of a city by storm. The rabble roared with all their throats, "Bring out the Canorum! Where is the Canorum?" (An unmeaning word which the Cornish generally used instead of Methodist.) Away went all the hinges at once, and the door fell back into the room. I stepped forward at once into the midst of them, and said, 'Here I am. Which of you has anything to say to me? To which of you have I done any wrong? To you? Or you? Or you?' I continued speaking… and, as far as the sound reached, the people were still; till one or two of their captains turned about and swore that not a man should touch him. Mr Thomas, a clergyman, then came up and asked, 'Are you not ashamed to use a stranger thus?' He was soon seconded by two or three gentlemen of the town, and one of the aldermen; with whom I walked down the town, speaking all the time, till I came to Mrs Maddern's house."

Fearing that the mob might cause more trouble his friends sent him on his horse and then smuggled him through a house that backed on to the waterfront. It is possible that the house was in East Street (a house there dates back to c 1685).

Ten years later he visited Pendennis Castle. He expressed the view that, "It might be made exceeding strong, but our wooden castles are sufficient."

^ Pendennis Castle

He visited Falmouth again in 1770 and preached near the church. His final visit was in 1789 when he preached "on top of a smooth topped hill", this could have been Pike's Hill above the church, and not far from where a residential care home for the elderly is now run by Methodist Homes for the Aged (MHA Care Group) in Arwenack Avenue.

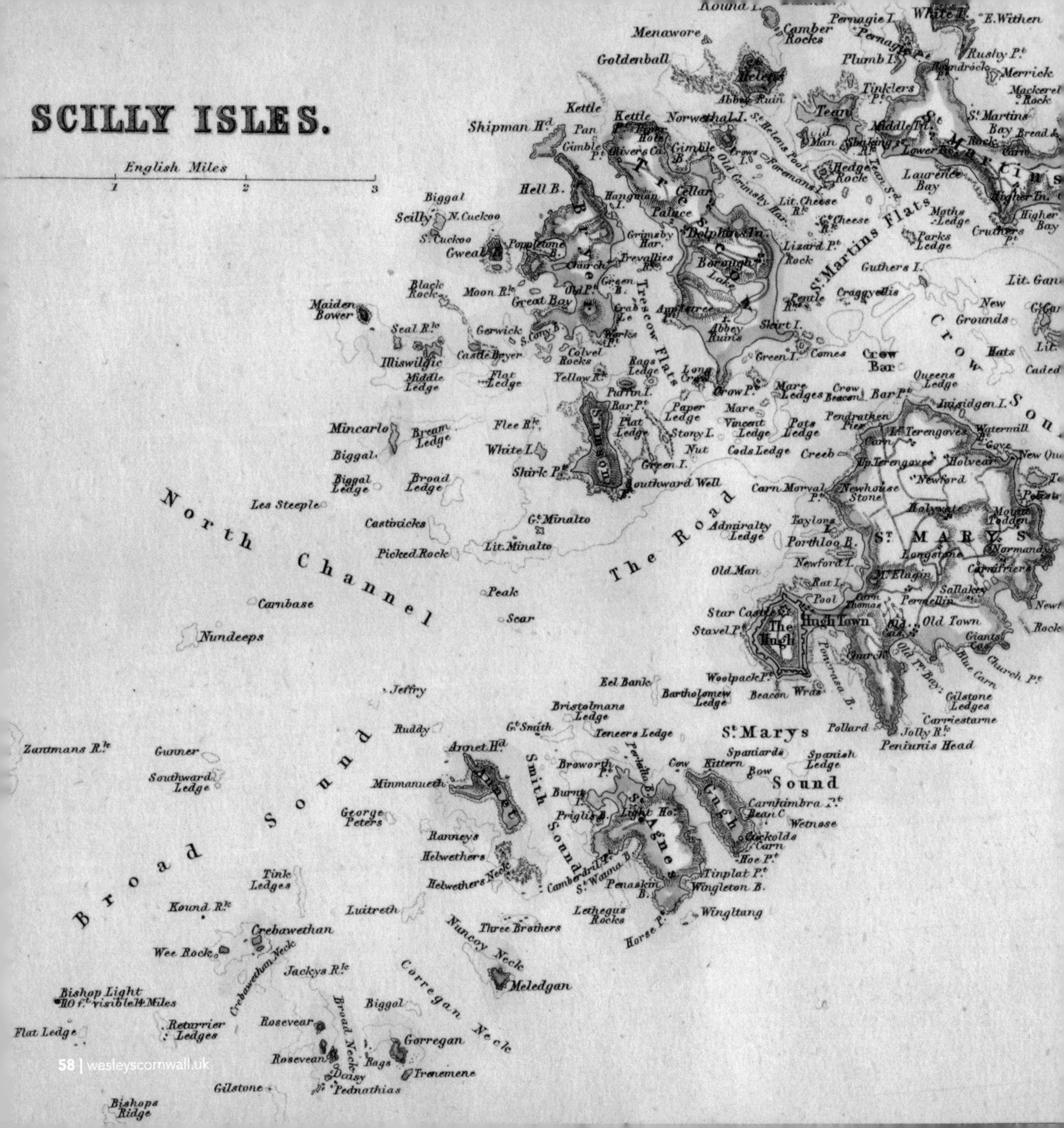
SCILLY ISLES.
English Miles
1
2
3
Round I.
Menawore
Camber Rocks
Pernagie I.
White I.
E. Withen
Goldenball
Helens
Plumb I.
Rushy Pt
Merrick
Mackerel Rock
Abbey Ruin
Tinklers Pt.
Tean
Kettle
Shipman Hd
Pan
Gimble Pt.
Kettle Pt.
Norwethal I.
St. Helens Pool
Olivers Ca.
Gimble B.
Crows I.
Old Grimsby Har.
Foremans I.
Hedge Rock
St. Martins Bay
Lower Tn.
Laurence Bay
Higher Tn.
Higher Bay
Crulhers Pt.
Hell B.
Hangman I.
Cellar
Palace
Lit. Cheese Rk
Gt. Cheese Rk
Moths Ledge
Parks Ledge
Biggal
Scilly
N. Cuckoo
S. Cuckoo
Gweal I.
Popplestone B.
Bryer
Church
Grimsby Har.
Dolphins Tn.
Trevallies Rk
Borough
Lake
Tresco
Lizard Pt.
Rock
St. Martins Flats
Guthers I.
Lit. Gan
Black Rock
Moon Rk
Great Bay
Old Pt.
Green B.
Tresco Flats
Crab Le
Pentle Rk
Craggyellis
New Grounds
Maiden Bower
Seal Rk
Gerwick
S. Cony B.
Works Pt.
Abbey Ruins
Skirt I.
Crow
Illiswilgic
Castle Bryer
Colvel Rocks
Rags Ledge
Green I.
Comes
Crow Bar
Hats
Lit.
Caded
Middle Ledge
Flat Ledge
Yellow Rk
Long Cr.
Mare Ledges
Crow Beacon
Bar Pt.
Queens Ledge
Crow Sound
Puffin I.
Crow Pt.
Innisidgen I.
Mincarlo
Bream Ledge
Flee Rk
Bar Pt.
Flat Ledge
Paper Ledge
Mare
Vincent Ledge
Pots Ledge
Pendrathen Pier
Lr. Terengoves
Watermill Cove
Biggal
White I.
Samson
Stony I.
Nut
Cods Ledge
Creeb
Up. Terengoves
Holvear
New Quay
Biggal Ledge
Broad Ledge
Shirk Pt.
Green I.
Southward Well
Carn Morval Pt.
Newhouse Stone
Newford
Les Steeple
North Channel
Castinicks
Gt. Minalto
The Road
Admiralty Ledge
Taylors I.
Porthloo B.
Holy Vale
Mount Todden
St. Marys
Picked Rock
Lit. Minalto
Old Man
Newford I.
Longstone
Normandy
Carnfriers
Mt. Flagin
Rat I.
Pool
Sallakey
Carnbase
Peak
Scar
Star Castle
Carn Thomas
Pernellin
Hugh Town
Old Town
Stavel Pt.
The Hugh
Nundeeps
Giants Cas.
Rock
Church
Old Tn. Bay
Blue Carn
Church Pt.
Porthcressa B.
Eel Bank
Woolpack Pt.
Bartholomew Ledge
Beacon
Wras
Gilstone Ledges
Jeffry
Bristolmans Ledge
Carriestarne
Jolly Rk
Ruddy
Gt. Smith
Teneers Ledge
St. Marys Sound
Pollard
Peninnis Head
Zantmans Rk
Gunner
Annet Hd
Smith Sound
Broworth Pt.
Cow
Kittern
Spaniards
Spanish Ledge
Bow
Southward Ledge
Minmanueth
Annet
Periglis B.
Burnt I.
Gugh
Carn Irinbra Pt.
Bean C
Wetnose
George Peters
Light Ho.
St. Agnes
Ranneys
Cuckolds Carn
Helwethers
Hoe Pt.
Broad Sound
Camberdril Pt.
St. Warna B.
Tinplat Pt.
Wingleton B.
Tink Ledges
Helwethers Neck
Penaskin B.
Kound Rk
Luitreth
Lethegus Rocks
Wingltang
Three Brothers
Horse Pt.
Crebawethan
Nuncoy Neck
Wee Rock
Crebawethan Neck
Jackys Rk
Meledgan
Corregan Neck
Bishop Light
110 ft. visible 14 Miles
Biggal
Retarrier Ledges
Rosevear
Broad Neck
Gorregan
Flat Ledge
Rosevean
Rags
Daisy
Tremene
Gilstone
Pednathias
Bishops Ridge

SIXTH PILGRIMAGE
THE ISLES OF SCILLY

As far as we know John only visited the Isles of Scilly once. On Monday 12 September 1743, after preaching that evening in St Ives, he wrote, "I had for some time a great desire to go and publish the love of God our Saviour, if it were but for one day, in the Isles of Scilly". He had mentioned his desire to some of his friends, so they arranged for him to sail the next day from St Ives, in the mayor's boat. He preached that evening on the Island of St Mary's and then at 5am and 9am before sailing back against a strong wind. The pilot of the boat said that they would need good luck to reach the land. John wrote, "But he knew not whom the winds and seas obey". They landed safely, but John's impression of the island was that it was, "Barren and dreary".

You can sail from Penzance in the morning and return later in the day. We trust that the impression it leaves will not be the same as John's.

JOHN WESLEY PREACHING TO
CORNISH 'TINNERS' AT TREWINT

SEVENTH PILGRIMAGE
ISBELL COTTAGE TREWINT

Isbell Cottage was a regular stopping off point for John as he travelled into Cornwall and before he tackled Bodmin Moor. The cottage belonged to Digory and Elizabeth Isbell who, inspired by the account of Elisha and the Shunammite woman (2 Kings 4:8–10), built two rooms onto their small cottage specifically for John and other itinerant preachers who passed by on their way to the rest of Cornwall. John was welcomed there at least six times between 1743 and 1762. He regularly preached at the cottage, and in July 1745 he made this appraisal, "Indeed I never remember so great awakening in Cornwall, wrought in so short a time, among young and old, rich and poor, from Trewint quite to the sea side."

Here is an opportunity to see the rooms where John prayed and slept, walk through the porch from which John and others preached, and imagine the 18th century scene.

< Artists impression of John Preaching outside the Isbell's cottage (picture courtesy of Trewint Cottage)

CORNWALL
A Pilgrim's Journal

RETURNING HOME

If the traffic, the distance, or the potholes that lay before you cause concern, take heart from the way John met perilous travelling conditions.

There was an occasion when he was travelling in a carriage near the sea. The tide was coming in quickly as they began to cross the sands. The driver of the carriage and a nearby sea captain thought it too dangerous to proceed, but John was determined to get to his preaching appointment. At the most dangerous point of the journey the horses were swimming and the carriage wheels were submerging into deep ruts. They were on the verge of being swept into the sea, but John looked calmly from the window of the carriage and being undisturbed by the peril reassured the driver that they would not sink. They arrived safely, very wet, but with the driver declaring, "It was a miracle…"

And, remember it took John six days to get back to London!

On the building: **PRIMITIVE METHODIST CHURCH 1831**

Sign on wall:

WELCOME TO
FORE STREET
METHODIST CHURCH

SUNDAY SERVICES
10.45am & 6.00pm
JUNIOR CHURCH
10.45am

WEEKDAY MEETINGS
FOR ALL AGES

We Worship
Jesus Christ as Lord

PASTOR R.ORR
Tel: 01736 798530

< One of many
chapels in St Ives

Wesley's CORNWALL

A Pilgrim's Journal

METHODISM

METHODISM

1791	Wesleyan Methodist Connexion	*Continued to the joining together to form The Methodist Church of Great Britain in 1932 (70,000 UK members in 1791)*
1797	Methodist New Connexion	*Joined with Bible Christians in 1907*
1806	Independent Methodists	*Continue to be independent. Name changed to Independent Methodist Connexion of Churches in 1898*
1811	Primitive Methodist Connexion	*Continued to the joining together to form The Methodist Church of Great Britain in 1932*
1815	Bible Christians	*Continued to the joining together to form The Methodist Church of Great Britain in 1932*
1827	Protestant Methodists	*Joined with the United Methodist Churches in 1836*
1832	Arminian Methodists	*Joined with the United Methodist Churches in 1837*
1836	Wesleyan Methodist Association	*Joined with the United Methodist Churches in 1836*
1849	Wesleyan Reformers	*Continue to be independent. Name changed to Wesleyan Reform Union in 1859*
1907	United Methodist Church	*Continued to the joining together to form The Methodist Church of Great Britain in 1932*
1932	The Methodist Church of Great Britain	*Formed by the Primitive Methodist Connexion, Wesleyan Methodist Connexion and Bible Christians*

In the eighteenth century the word "Methodist" was aimed unkindly at any person or group of fundamentalists. It was a derogatory term used along with "Bible Moths" by scoffers against any who dared to step outside of the established Christian traditions.

Jesus said, "If the world hates you, keep in mind that it hated me first."

Paul lists the sorts of hardships that may afflict the servants of God (2 Corinthians 6:10). It would be easy to ascribe dramatic church growth to people like Paul and John Wesley, they both endured suffering albeit in different centuries. However, just as Paul did not work and bear harsh treatment alone, neither did John. There were many who worked and suffered as John did, unsung heroes of the Faith. Some joined him in his ministry and others like Howell Harris, the Welsh revivalist, were all instrumental in advancing the Kingdom and Methodism.

As an ordained Anglican Minister John had always been keen to ensure that Methodism should not replace the established Church. Methodism only emerged as a separate entity around the time of his death in 1791. He had always encouraged converts to attend their local parish church.

Nevertheless, he was banned from many churches and some Ministers actively encouraged the crowds to intimidate, abuse and rail against him.

Wesleyan Methodists – the formal designation of 'the people called Methodists, in the connexion established by John Wesley' came to be shortened to 'Wesleyan Methodists' or simply 'Wesleyans' to distinguish this group from others. In the first half of the nineteenth century the Wesleyan movement grew rapidly. By its centenary in 1839 the denomination claimed over 400,000 members and an institutional infrastructure to match: thousands of chapels, large and small; day and Sunday schools; a Missionary Society for work overseas; an array of publications; and an army of volunteers serving the Connexion as chapel trustees, local preachers, stewards, class leaders and Sunday school teachers. John Wesley's small band of 'travelling preachers' had become Wesleyan ministers.

A fund was launched in 1898 to raise "a million guineas from a million Methodists". The appeal had raised nearly £1,076,000 by 1904, which was used to build chapels and schools, and to support overseas mission, temperance work and children's homes, as well as to build Westminster Central Hall in London (opened in 1912) as a national centre for the Wesleyan Methodist Connexion.

Methodist New Connexion – In West Cornwall it was formed from the Teetotal Methodists. Teetotal Street remains in St Ives to this day. There were Teetotal Methodists in Truro, St Ives, Penzance and Cambourne.

Independent Methodists – The Independent Methodist Connexion is a group of churches which are situated in the North of England. Each church is self-governing. There are today, around 1500 members meeting in around 70 churches.

Primitive Methodist Connexion – "Primitive" meant "simple" or "relating to an original stage"; the Primitive Methodists saw themselves as practicing a purer form of Christianity, closer to the earliest Methodists. They were initially established in the mining areas. The denomination still continues in parts of America.

Bible Christians – A large proportion of the Methodist Church in Cornwall grew from the Bible Christian denomination. A Bible Christian Chapel can still be found in St Peters Street St Ives. They have been described as a "West Country sort of Methodism". They existed from 1815 to 1907. Billy Bray (1794 to 1868) was the most famous Bible Christian. He called himself "The King's Son".

Protestant Methodists – Also known as 'Ranters', for their enthusiastic preaching, 'Primitive' Methodists were so called because they wanted a return to an earlier, purer form of Methodism, as founded by John Wesley, based on the early church.

Arminian Methodists – Although these Arminian Methodists claimed to be faithfully following John Wesley's teaching on entire sanctification, in fact they departed from Wesley's strong emphasis on salvation by repentance and faith. They turned saving faith into merely believing that Christ died for sinners and their doctrine of human response was almost a belief that original sin did not taint human nature and that mortal will is still capable of choosing good or evil without special Divine aid.

Wesleyan Methodist Association - Formed, largely by Protestant Methodists. Their place of worship was the Wesleyan Association Chapel. They sent several missionaries to Jamaica and Australia.

Wesleyan Reformers - Since 1849, Wesleyan Reformers have maintained their witness as a separate body among the Free churches. The point of difference with Wesleyan Methodism was that of church governance, an autonomous form of government being desired in which each church has the right of administering its own affairs.

United Methodist Church – A denomination called the United Methodist Church was created in America on April 23, 1968, when The Evangelical United Brethren Church and The Methodist Church united to form a new denomination, now comprising 18 million members, but the original denomination in the UK of the same name merged with The Methodist Church of Great Britain in 1932.

The Methodist Church of Great Britain - Many of the 188,000 Methodists meeting in the 4,512 churches in the UK now meet under the joint name of The Methodist Church in Britain, but that was not the case up until 1932.

You will see that in St Ives there are many chapels with either Methodist or Wesley in their name. Not only did Methodism form as a separate denomination from the Church of England but it also divided within itself. There are estimated to be between 60 and 80 million Methodists worldwide. John once famously said, "The world is my parish."

"My fear is not that our great movement, known as the Methodists, will eventually cease to exist or one day die from the earth. My fear is that our people will become content to live without the fire, the power, the excitement, the supernatural element that makes us great."

John Wesley

BENEDICTION

Now, to God the Father, who first loved us,
and made us accepted in the Beloved;
to God the Son, who loved us, and washed
us from our sins in his own blood;
to God the Holy Ghost, who sheddeth the
love of God abroad in our hearts, be all love
and all glory in time and to all eternity.

Amen.

Benediction by John Wesley

"Show me your ways, LORD, teach me your paths."

Psalm 25:4

Wesley's

CORNWALL

A Pilgrim's Journal

MY LIFE JOURNAL

God was with John in all his trials and accomplishments. He is the ever-present God who is similarly with us in our life's journey today. He is the same yesterday and today and forever

Hebrews 13:8

As we give careful thought to the phrase, "The best of all, God is with us!", what has that meant for you in the past and present and what could it mean for the future?

John, and many others of his era, wrote an account of their lives in journals. We would not be considering the life of John Wesley in the same way today had he not committed to paper the story of his life, and the church, as they advanced. He often just reflected on the day's events.

Here is an opportunity for you to prayerfully write down significant events in your life story over the whole of your life, in recent years or months, or even this week. It will undoubtedly reassure you of God's providence and care, for he has said, "Never will I leave you, never will I forsake you."

25804294R00054

Printed in Poland
by Amazon Fulfillment
Poland Sp. z o.o., Wrocław